TRUMP
Über Alles*

*All over everything

Other books by David Hedges

Petty Frogs on the Potomac (1997)
The Wild Bunch (1998)
Brother Joe (2000)
*Steens Mountain Sunrise: Poems
of the Northern Great Basin* (2004)
Selected Sonnets (2006)
*A Funny Thing Happened on My Way
to a Geology Degree* (2011)
*Prospects of Life After Birth:
Memoir in Poetry and Prose* (2019)
The Changer (2021)

TRUMP
Über Alles

Rhymes for Trying Times

David Hedges

Road's End Press

Trump Über Alles
Poetry
David Hedges

Copyright © 2022 David Hedges

FIRST EDITION

All rights reserved. No part of this book may be reproduced in any manner without the express written consent of the author or Road's End Press except for brief excerpts in reviews and articles.

Thanks to the editors of *Light: A Journal of Light Verse,* for publishing many of these poems.

Road's End Press
326 Pearl Street
Oregon City, Oregon 97045

To order copies, visit roadsendpress.com

Cover art by Jim Agpalza
Author photo by Gavin Sterrett
Layout, design, and typography by Andrew Hedges
Proofreading by Valerie Witte

Library of Congress Control Number: 2022901723

ISBN: 978-1-7366102-2-0

Ebook version available

Printed in the United States of America

*I dedicate this book
to the U.S. Constitution, the Bill of Rights,
and the rule of law.*

Table of Contents

x   Preface

xii   Cast of Characters

I   "Part of the beauty of me is that I'm very rich."

3   A Shot in the Dark
4   Snow White and the Seven Dwarfs
6   A Picture Worth a Thousand Words
7   Slapstick
8   The Trump Family Circus
9   Dream Fight: Charles Koch Vs. Donald Trump
10   In Praise of Billionaires
11   But Does It Pass the Scrabble Test?
12   Baby on Board

II   "I think apologizing is great, but…"

15   The CEO of POTUS, Inc.
16   Bolton Bombs the Boob
17   Ivanka's Blooming Blunder
18   "Let's go with guidelines"
19   Your Tax Dollars at Work
20   Farmer Don
21   Highland Bull
22   Burning Questions

III "I am the Chosen One."

25   Apocalypse Now
26   Paul's Epistles to His Apostles
27   Two Balliol Rhymes
28   Let's Make a Deal
30   The Four Horsemen of the Pandemic
31   The Donald's Grand Distraction
33   The Magic Orb
34   Par for the Course
35   L'État, C'est Trump
36   Ways & Means

IV "I'm highly educated. I know words."

- 39 O Commandant! My Commandant!
- 40 The Tao of D'oh
- 41 Six Pack
- 42 On Giving the Wall the Gate
- 44 Yodeling All the Way
- 45 Double Whammy
- 46 Breaking Wind
- 47 The Devil's in the Details
- 48 Making Mockery Great Again
- 49 Vicente for Presidente
- 50 The Wily Gerrymander

V "I am a very stable genius."

- 53 "What I Love" by Donnie Trump
- 54 Shaking Hands
- 55 Little Donnie's Really Big Parade
- 56 Bombs Away
- 57 A Quartet of Quatrains
- 58 The Donald Prepares Coast Guard Academy Cadets…
- 59 A Trio of Limericks with Titles
- 60 Top Priority
- 61 Little Donnie's Very Bad Dream
- 62 Hair Apparent

VI "The worst thing a man can do is go bald."

- 65 Doctor No
- 67 Doctor Maybe
- 68 Doctor Yes
- 69 Is Donnie Really Bald on Top?
- 70 U.S. and Russia Revive Cold War Game…
- 71 CNN Poll
- 72 Vlad the Impaler
- 73 Meanwhile, in a Galaxy Far, Far Away…
- 74 The Coronavirus Conspiracy
- 75 For Your Eyes Only
- 76 Trumpster Diving

77   The Ho-Humness of Donald's Misdeeds
78   Presidential Kiss-off
79   A Tale of Two Tyrants
80   Meathead

VII   "All the women on The Apprentice flirted..."

83   The Devil's Apprentice
84   The Dog Daze of August
85   The United States Cheerleader Squad
86   Stormy Blows the Whistle
87   Stormy Blather
88   Ménage à Trois
89   Polish Two-step
90   Making America Itch Again

VIII   "I love the poorly educated."

93   Whiteboards from Hell
94   Manafort's Manifest Millions
95   A Trio of Bobbleheads
96   The Great Prevaricator
97   Rudy Giuliani
98   Bad Penny
99   Three-fingered Giuliani
100 Inartful Dodger
101 Conspiracy Theories
102 Nightmare on Downing Street
103 The Dumb and the Dumber

105 **Author's Notes**

Preface

All but a very few of these poems were written in response to an invitation to submit to a weekly competition sponsored by *Light: A Journal of Light Verse*. I plunged in and began writing two topical poems every week. Weeks turned into months, months into years.

More often than not, I had the 45th President of the United States squarely in my literary sights. He begged and pleaded to be satirized, parodied, and skewered. No character since Shakespeare's Falstaff has been so ripe for ridicule, and so prone to pratfalls. No political figure in American history has boasted such a broad and deep assemblage of unsavory and unscrupulous associates.

Take Felix Sater, Russian mobster and close business associate of Trump, who in 2015 emailed Michael Cohen, Trump's attorney and fixer: "Our boy can become president of the USA and we can engineer it. I will get all of Putin's team to buy in on this."

It became clear to me that Trump won by cheating when he began attacking the voting process. Every accusation he has ever hurled has been a clear deflection from identical misbehavior. The purpose of this infantile tactic is to brand anyone who accuses him of cheating, or of any wrongdoing, as a kindergarten copycat.

While I was writing these poems, frustration grew as I watched Trump shred the U.S. Constitution, batter the Bill of Rights, run roughshod over our nation's institutions, and, thanks to Fox News, convince tens of millions of Americans to abandon time-honored principles and swallow his poppycock. I felt utterly helpless.

Trump Über Alles is my reaction to the threat of Trump's blatant attempt to mold a fascist dictatorship in America. He has sent his goon squads into the streets. He has stripped government agencies of their ability to carry out legislative mandates. He has knocked the teeth from regulations aimed at protecting ordinary people.

His first wife, Ivana, told that the only book he kept on his nightstand was a collection of Adolf Hitler's speeches. We have seen how he has cozied up with autocrats around the world and insulted traditional democratic allies.

Americans today think of fascism as something that happened in the last century in Germany and Italy. We tend to forget the German American Bund and the prominent people, such as Henry

Ford and Charles Lindbergh, who openly supported the Nazi Party.

In 1935, Nobel Laureate Sinclair Lewis published *It Can't Happen Here,* a novel in which fascists rise to power in America. This was during the period when the Bund was staging public rallies and parades. In a recent reading, I was struck by similarities between the nationalistic fervor of Germany in the 1930s and that being whipped up around us by would-be dictator Donald Trump.

Huey Long, who served as U.S. Senator from Louisiana from 1932 until his assassination in 1935, is credited with authoring the statement, "When fascism comes to America, it will be wrapped in the flag and carrying a cross."

Think of Trump hugging the flag at the 2019 CPAC convention, a meme that's grown into a cottage industry. Or Trump holding a Bible and babbling incoherently in front of the handiest church after threatening military action against protestors. Outrageous hypocrisy.

Trump praised the invasion of Ukraine by Vladimir Putin, a fascist tyrant, dubbing it *genius* and *savvy* and *smart*. Brain-dead Republicans swallowed his poison! Putin and Trump—birds of a feather.

I'll leave you with this notion. Laughter has the potential to deflate Trump as surely as Dorothy's bucket of water melted the Wicked Witch of the West. Pour it out! Pay attention to his idiotic words and actions. Share jokes on social media and with relatives, friends, and neighbors, even complete strangers.

Show Trump for the utter buffoon he is, a know-nothing-say-anything embarrassment to America in the eyes of the world.

Up with democracy! Down with Trump!

David Hedges
Oregon City, Oregon
March 5, 2022

Cast of Characters (in order of appearance)

I

Donald J. Trump, former Republican POTUS
Melania Trump, former FLOTUS
Kayleigh McEnany, Trump's former press secretary
Rudy Giuliani, Trump's attorney & trained monkey
Mike Pence, Trump's former Vice President
Betsy DeVos, Trump's former Education Secretary
Dr. Anthony Fauci, White House medical advisor
Mitch McConnell, Republican Senate Minority Leader
Ivanka Trump, Trump's daughter & intimate advisor
Jared Kushner, Trump's son-in-law & oafish advisor
Monty Python, silly & surreal British comedy troupe
Joe Biden, Democratic POTUS
Barack Obama, former Democratic POTUS
Larry, Moe, and Curly Joe, The Three Stooges
Atilla the Hun, ruler of the Hunnic Empire
Donald Trump, Jr., Trump's older son & witless advisor
Eric Trump, Trump's other son & Fox News guest
Charles Koch, billionaire & libertarian conspirator
Paul Ryan, former Republican House Speaker
Ronald Reagan, former Republican POTUS

II

John Bolton, Trump's former United Nations envoy
Crown Prince MBS, Saudi Arabian despot & Trump crony
Hillary Clinton, Democratic candidate for President
King George III, British monarch & Trump's alter ego
Chuck Schumer, Democratic Senate Majority Leader
Nancy Pelosi, Democratic House Speaker
Xi Jinping, President of the People's Republic of China
Vladimir Putin, President of Russia & Trump crony
John Bel Edwards, Democratic Governor of Louisiana
Andrew Vernon, contributor for *The Hill*

III

Rev. Franklin Graham, evangelical huckster
Jesus Christ, first-century Jewish preacher & religious leader
Ayn Rand, late author & goddess of the rabid right
Paula White, Trump's screwball former spiritual advisor
Callista Gingrich, former Ambassador to the Holy See
Pope Francis, Catholic pontiff & ruler of Vatican City
Newt Gingrich, former Republican House Speaker
Bill Clinton, former Democratic POTUS
Monica Lewinsky, former White House intern
Steven Miller, Trump's former political advisor
Mike Pompeo, Trump's former Secretary of State
William Barr, Trump's former Attorney General
Zdravko Krivokapić, Prime Minister of Montenegro
Emmanuel Macron, President of France
Binyamin Netanyahu, former Israeli Prime Minister
P.T. Barnum, 19th-century showman & hoaxster
King Kong, giant gorilla & Hollywood film star
Chucky, serial killer & Hollywood film star
Cheech & Chong, award-winning comedy duo
The Cheshire Cat, known for its mischievous grin
Tiger Woods, professional golfer
Alan Dershowitz, Trump's notorious celebrity attorney

IV

Robert Mueller, leader of Trump-Russia investigation
Sauli Niinistö, President of Finland
Vicente Fox, former President of Mexico

V

Sean Hannity, Fox News rabble rouser & Trump crony
Theresa May, former British Prime Minister
Shinzō Abe, former Japanese Prime Minister
Michael Cohen, Trump's former attorney & jailed fixer
Socrates, Greek philosopher & politician, put to death
The Red Queen, famous for "Off with his head!"
Tucker Carlson, Fox News rabble rouser & Trump crony

VI

Dr. Harold Bornstein, Trump's former personal physician
Dr. Ronny Jackson, former Physician to the President
Dr. Sean Conley, Trump's final White House Physician

VII

Omarosa, *The Apprentice* star & former Trump aide
Stormy Daniels, porn star & former Trump sex object
Kim Jong-un, North Korean dictator & Trump crony
Gen. John Kelly, Trump's former Chief of Staff
Roseanne Barr, loud-mouthed right-wing TV actor
Jackie, Roseanne's wimpy liberal TV sister
Dan, Roseanne's hapless nonpartisan TV husband
Agata Kornhauser-Duda, wife of the Polish President

VIII

Steve Bannon, Trump's former chief political strategist
Paul Manafort, Trump's former lawyer & jailbird
James Comey, Trump's former FBI Director
Jeff Sessions, Trump's former Attorney General
Orin Hatch, former Utah Republican Senator
Sean Spicer, Trump's former press secretary & dancer
Lindsey Graham, South Carolina Republican Senator
Boris Johnson, British Prime Minister
Jean-Paul Sarte, French existentialist & author
Mr. Bean, British TV character
Elizabeth II, British Monarch
Grigori Rasputin, Russian mystic & charlatan
Wilbur Ross, Trump's former Secretary of Commerce

I

*"Part of the beauty of me is that
I am very rich."*

A Shot in the Dark

> "Maybe we'll give that a shot..."
> —Donald J. Trump, Dictator-in-Waiting

His Worship has an itch to make
Himself our "President for Life."
If China can, for heaven's sake,
Why not America? His wife

Deserves a title, too: "Her Grace,
The Empress of the Universe."
And how about that poker face
Whose every word's a curse, or worse?

For brevity, let's call him "Vice,"
Since virtue's surely not his forte.
And "Justice" isn't quite precise
For members of the Highest Court,

Mostly white men wearing robes
The color of the blackest night,
And mostly flaming homophobes
Who idolize the rabid right.

The lily-livered ding-a-lings
Who shamelessly parade their sins
While pulling House and Senate strings
Shall now be called "The Evil Twins."

And best we give the nepotites
Who share the eyes and ears of God
A title fit for socialites:
"The Heirs of Avarice and Fraud."

Snow White and the Seven Dwarfs

> "Dopey annoys Grumpy and Doc on a consistent basis."
> —Wikipedia

Snow White Kayleigh

First thing she did was give the press
Her word that "I will never lie."
Four minutes later, more or less,
She did, and didn't bat an eye.

Bashful Rudy

Did Giuliani disappear
Or simply quench his quest for fame?
If he got tossed out on his ear,
Assume that Dopey Don's to blame.

Grumpy Mike

The Brothers Grimm had Pence in mind
When dreaming Grumpy up. His heart
Is cold, his ears are deaf, he's blind
And can't stand women, for a start.

Happy Betsy

Hard starboard is the course she steers
As first mate on the Ship of Fools.
If Dopey Don gets four more years
She'll do away with public schools.

Doc Anthony

He's something of a White House pest,
Since only Dopey Don knows where
And when and why to test,
And how to beat Obamacare.

Sneezy Mitch

He runs his Punch and Judy show
With buggy whip and monkey wrench.
He claims his Russian quid pro quo
Is quite all right, despite the stench.

Evil Queen Ivanka

She spends her time invoking spells
Intended to conceal her wealth.
Her offshore fortune swells and swells,
Though cluelessness reveals her stealth.

Crown Prince Jared

He knows enough to know he knows
Enough to know he's always right,
And so, like Monty Python, goes
Clip-clopping off, an errant knight.

Dopey Don

He pulls a Joker from his sleeve
When no one blessed with common sense
Would in a million years believe
That anyone could be so dense.

Sleepy Joe

His numbers show it pays to hunker
Like vintage wine upon a shelf,
Sequestered in a basement bunker
While Dopey Don destroys himself.

Barack, the Magic Mirror

He knows what Dopey Don wants most:
To reign upon a golden throne,
To lay to rest his Daddy's ghost,
And boost his low testosterone.

A Picture Worth a Thousand Words

   "The Pure American Banality of Donald Trump's
   White House Fast-Food Banquet"
   —*The New Yorker*

As Lincoln ponders on the wall
Above the splendid venue,
Little Donnie stands in thrall
At having planned the menu—

The silly snicker on his face,
The tiny hands splayed out,
The table stacked beyond disgrace
With boxes filled, he touts,

With Big Macs, fries, Filet-O-Fishes
Enough to feed an army,
Calories beyond all wishes.
Donnie's gone plumb barmy.

"Look at me," he spouts with glee,
"I've scored another coup!"
The Clemson Tigers take a knee.
Chacun à son goût.

Slapstick

Little Donnie's a barrel of fun,
Three Stooges all rolled into one,
Though his "Art of the Deal"
Stressing lie, cheat, and steal
Out-plunders Attila the Hun.

The Trump Family Circus

The clown car appears to be stuck in reverse,
And Ringmaster Donnie can't think what to do
But tweet hissy fits and relentlessly curse
As bozos bail out—oh, and call it a coup.

Ivanka, aloft in her glittering tights,
Sails on through thin air with the greatest of ease,
Expanding her graft to incomparable heights
By putting the squeeze on her well-heeled Chinese.

Don's son-in-law, Jared, loan-juggler supreme,
Plays footsie with Salman, the Saudi crown prince,
And kowtows to Putin's despotic regime
As qualified diplomats grimace and wince.

Rudolfo, the screwball Ukrainian freak,
Reprises the guiles in his vast repertoire,
A sideshow replete with the president's clique
Of bootlicking sycophants, starring Bill Barr.

While Mitch cracks his whip in the off-center ring,
Republicans circle, performing their rounds,
Attached, trunk to tail, in an unbroken string,
Unable to utter articulate sounds.

Don Junior and Eric spout off on talk shows—
Imperious ham-handed rich little kids
Defending dear Daddy, whose nose grows and grows,
With plenteous pro quos and copious quids.

Dream Fight: Charles Koch Vs. Donald Trump

Break out the popcorn and the lemonade—
The Battle of the Billionaires is on!
Charles first lobbed a verbal hand grenade,
Then Donald answered at the crack of dawn,

Bombarding Charles with rapid-fire tweets.
At issue: Who will rule the GOP?
Envision proxies taking to the streets
And interns chasing trustees up a tree.

Charles will win the party's heart and soul.
Trump's house of cards is built on shifting sands.
Progressive Democrats will take control.
Envision everybody shaking hands.

So much for fantasy. Down in the muck,
The Donald doesn't worry who he screws.
The Brothers Koch don't give a rusty fuck.
No matter who comes out on top, we lose.

In Praise of Billionaires

You have to hand it to the billionaires
Or they will send their minions round to take it.
They write the rules: Whatever's yours is theirs,

What's theirs is stashed offshore to make it
Vanish when the taxman comes to call.
The burden falls on you who cannot fake it

With loopholes, credits, and deferrals, all
Designed to guarantee that no one shares
The wealth who's not already made a haul.

But Does It Pass the Scrabble Test?

> "Had America not absorbed the sheer skeeviness
> of that decade, we wouldn't be where we are today."
> —Op-Ed, *The New York Times*

It seems that skeeviness is now
A word that everyone should know;
The New York Times would not allow
A word to interrupt the flow

Its readers are accustomed to
When tapping into current news.
Did skeevy pass a peer review?
Was it intended to amuse?

If skeeviness means what I think,
It started in the reign of Ronald,
When everything began to stink,
And culminated in The Donald.

Baby on Board

As Trump took off for Liechtenstein
To buff his image, have some fun,
The yellow diamond caution sign
Shone from the door of Air Force One.

II

"I think apologizing's a great thing, but you have to be wrong. I will absolutely apologize, sometime in the hopefully distant future, if I'm ever wrong."

The CEO of POTUS, Inc.

> "The Trump Organization Ordered Golf Course Markers With the Presidential Seal. That May Be Illegal."
> —*ProPublica,* March 5, 2018

> [On March 6, after the exposé, the Trump Organization withdrew the markers and said someone else had ordered them, a claim disputed by the manufacturer. Federal law forbids the use of the seal for anything but official government business, with fines and imprisonment of up to six months.]

> "I have said for a long time we need a businessman in the White House."
> —Tweet by candidate Trump, May 20, 2015

A Senate Bill has been proposed to deal
With how and where the Presidential Seal
May legally be used. Once they repeal
Obamacare and reinvent the wheel,
And leaders Ryan and McConnell feel
The measure has widespread-enough appeal,
Republicans will bow their heads and kneel.

Bolton Bombs the Boob

John Bolton's takedown offers proof
That nothing's ever as it seems
With Dopey Don—it's all a spoof,
A takeoff on his wildest dreams.

Since nothing's going on upstairs,
He puts faith in his trusty gut
To weigh what's best for billionaires,
And jumps on Fox News scuttlebutt.

When he learned how a quid pro quo
Could be of use in his campaign
To dig some dirt on Sleepy Joe,
He turned to China and Ukraine,

And Turkey, too—it's in the book,
Along with other sleazy details:
Why did reporters overlook
Ivanka's use of private emails?

Don sidetracked them with poppycock,
Absolving Crown Prince MBS
Of murder—not a major shock,
The way he messes with the press.

He doesn't do much else but tweet
Invectives at his foes, with John
His latest target—oh, and cheat
At golf, with people looking on!

Ivanka's Blooming Blunder

Her email caper chalks her up
As a copycat of Hillary.
Let's see if Daddy locks her up
Or sticks her in a pillory,

Or maybe simply docks her pay
As a token to democracy,
Or snickers as she talks her way
Around her gross hypocrisy.

"Let's go with guidelines"
  —Donald J. Trump, Leader of the Free World

Somebody must have whacked Dear Leader hard.
One day he claims to be King George the Third
Reincarnated. In a flash, he's tarred
And feathered. Suddenly the lines are blurred

As strict constructionists swoop in and pounce
Alongside those more liberally inclined.
Nobody's willing to bestow an ounce
Of credence on Dear Leader's frame of mind.

The next day, beaten to a pulp, he flips
His monumental belly flop and claims
He didn't mean what seemed to pass his lips—
"Authorize" was his intent. He blames

His standard cast of enemies, the Faux
News folks, the Democratic leaders Chuck
And Nancy, immigrants from Mexico—
It doesn't matter who, he'll pass the buck

Because, as everybody knows, he's not
Responsible for anything that might
Affect his reelection, though it's bought
And paid for. What if citizens unite

Behind Faux Biden and he gets the ax?
How will he ever show he's just as strong
As Xi and Vladimir? His income tax
Returns could pack him off to jail! What's wrong

With always being right? His fans adore
His swagger, blindly swallow all his lies.
His sacking of the Diplomatic Corps
Proves he fulfilled his promise to downsize.

Your Tax Dollars at Work

Twelve billion may sound like a hell of a lot
But double-down Donnie will tell you it's not—
Chump change to your run-of-the-mill oligarch.

That's all it will take to make farmers forget
He dried up their markets and ran up the debt,
Both theirs and the nation's, and all on a lark.

He promised us tariffs, and tariffs we got.
The whole world is doing it—who would've thought?
Not deal-maker Donnie, alone in the dark.

No matter, it's all in the hands of Dame Fate
Who's finding it difficult keeping things straight—
There's hunting in Yellowstone National Park?

Farmer Don

Big Mac Donald has a farm
And on his farm he has some cornfields
And in these cornfields he has some holes
And in these holes he has some poles
And on these poles he has some flags
And visitors with clubs and balls

With a putt-putt here, a putt-putt there
Here a putt, there a putt
Everywhere a putt-putt

Farmer Don plays alchemist
And takes your basic country club
And turns his tax accountants loose
And orders them to strut their stuff
And cut his payments to the bone
And voilà, turns his corn to gold

With a wink-wink here, a wink-wink there
Here a wink, there a wink
Everywhere a wink-wink

Highland Bull

The Donald's latest scandal trumps them all
(The Russian thing, the European slights)
In terms of sheer unmitigated gall.

He's been caught pinching assets, dead to rights,
Branding, with a stolen coat of arms,
Everything from socks to golf course sites.

In Scotland, that's a cinch to trip alarms
And tie some knickerbockers in a knot.
Officials say adulteration harms

The whole of heraldry, a topic fraught
With shalts and shalt nots of the strictest test.
The cause célèbre started when Trump bought

Mar-a-Lago from someone whose crest
Was part of the décor. He took it, chopped
"Integrity," the motto, kept the rest.

His Scottish permit application flopped:
"Ye cannae break th' rules!" The Donald chose
A new design. A pending suit was dropped.

His legal crest, a two-faced eagle, shows
The world his nature, mounted on a wall
At his Scottish golf resort. And so it goes.

Burning Questions

> "And as for the president: God bless his heart."
> —John Bel Edwards, whose reelection as Louisiana's Democratic governor the president had turned into a referendum on Donald Trump

> "Bless your heart," a phrase that can mean "You are dumb or otherwise impaired, but you can't help it."
> —Wikipedia

> "President Donald Trump visited Walter Reed National Medical Center due to chest discomfort."
> —Andrew Vernon, a contributor for *The Hill* who writes on veterans' issues

Did John Bel Edwards mean to curse
The president, or wish him well?
Backhanded praise is sometimes worse
Than simply yelling, "Go to hell!"

Did someone poke a Voodoo doll
With hatpins aimed at Donnie's heart?
Did Rudy's breach of protocol
And fabrications play a part?

Was Trump's discomfort nothing more
Than chronic acid indigestion,
Or was the Diplomatic Corps
To blame?—another burning question.

III

"I am the Chosen One."

Apocalypse Now

The son of Pastor Billy Graham declared
That evangelicals believe the Prez,
An ordinary mortal unimpaired
By any virtue he thus far has shared,
Is Jesus Christ. Or so the Bible says.

In Franklin's eyes, the Prez is plagued with sin,
But aren't we all? So cut the guy some slack.
The Ten Commandments take it on the chin
But immorality is mostly spin
By humanists and others of their claque.

Some folks maintain that he's a total fraud
And takes His name in vain to fool the flock.
So why do fundamentalists applaud
And view him as the second Son of God?
Abortion's done. The rest is poppycock.

Paul's Epistles to His Apostles

The Speaker has an evil streak.
He stripped the Chaplain of his post
For dissing right-wing doublespeak

On who needs tax relief the most,
The rich, the poor, the middle class.
(Praise him above, ye heavenly host—

This Chaplain knows his ass from grass!)
The Speaker, meantime, wanders lost,
The wrong end of his looking glass

Fixed on the future—double-crossed
By Ayn Rand, goddess of his youth,
Who preached a social holocaust.

The Chaplain spreads the gospel truth,
While Father, Son, and Holy Ghost
Will haunt Paul at the polling booth.

The Speaker has the gall to boast
Of shipping poor folks up the creek
As his own fortunes turn to toast.

Two Balliol Rhymes

1

My hallowed name is Paula White.
I'm God's Best Friend. I've seen His light
Up close. We two came face to face.
It's true. I visited His place,

His holy throne in Heaven on high,
Where angels taught me how to fly.
He sent me down to make Trump pray.
I don't come cheap. The people pay.

2

Giuliani is my name
And self-promotion is my game.
The human being I most admire?
It's me, you fool, so why inquire?

Remember, I'm the people's choice.
They love my face, adore my voice
As much as I do. On TV,
They never get enough of me.

Let's Make a Deal

As with every move The Donald's made,
His pick for envoy to the Holy See
Defies credulity. It's retrograde
To taunt the Pontiff with impiety.

Forethought ordains an envoy versed in God,
A diplomat whose creds are simon-pure.
Why did Callista Gingrich get the nod?
Was she the only soul he could procure,

A cinch to gain Republican acclaim?
The third and so far current wife of Newt,
The galoot who flipped and flopped his way to fame
As Speaker of the House of Ill Repute,

Callista was his mistress, an escape
From holy matrimony's bonds. The Pope
Is bound to have his nose bent out of shape.
What does The Donald take him for, a dope?

This Shepherd isn't one to fleece his flock
Or plunder nations to assuage caprice.
Unlike The Donald, Francis walks his talk
And has a pipeline to the Prince of Peace.

Is Trump rewarding Naughty Newt because
He flogged Bill Clinton for the escapade
With Monica (despite no broken laws),
While he himself played footsie with an aide,

None other than Callista? Their affair
Was overlooked upon The Hill, though why,
God only knows. (Why would reporters care,
When they had Bill, a bigger fish, to fry?)

Number Two was mistress when the first
Of Newt's three wives was licit. Number Four
Might well be waiting in the wings to burst
Upon the scene through Newt's revolving door.

This theory may illuminate the deal
Newt cut: "You send Callista off to Rome,
While I stay home and test my sex appeal.
She'll be content to climb Saint Peter's Dome."

The Four Horsemen of the Pandemic

> "Four die-hard loyalists are enabling Trump's apocalyptic coronavirus response. Kushner, Miller, Pompeo, and Barr are using the nation's greatest public health crisis in a century to foment hoaxes and punish the president's enemies."
> —*The Intercept*

With Judgment Day looming around the next bend,
It's rather surprising that Jesus would send
Four bumblers to Earth in a crazy clown car—
Kushner and Miller, Pompeo and Barr.

Of course, if His object is sparking distress,
These bozos snatch failure from certain success,
Competing to prove who's more foolish by far—
Kushner or Miller, Pompeo or Barr.

Their roles in the End Times are written in stone;
They do dirty deeds while the twit on the throne
Tweets with one hand in the grand cookie jar.
Kushner and Miller, Pompeo and Barr

Wreak havoc as no one before them can claim.
Though Nixon's four horsemen brought anger and shame,
Their actions seem piddling and not on a par
With Kushner and Miller, Pompeo and Barr.

The Donald's Grand Distraction

With no responsibilities
But showing up for photo ops,
Trump danced with princes to appease
The Saudi Arabs with his chops,

Then gave them billions more for arms,
And helicopters they'll construct,
As he fulfills a pledge and farms
New jobs abroad. Ivanka sucked

A cool one hundred million clams
For her new women's fund (a tithe),
But not one dime for mammograms
Or birth control. (She tends to writhe

When pressured to defend her haul.)
Then off to Israel so he
Could say he saw the Western Wall
And pad his campaign money tree.

(The look in Netanyahu's eyes
When Donald shouted, "Stop the show!"
And bragged about Israeli spies…)
Larry, Moe, and Curly Joe

Would be hard-pressed to match his style,
Part P.T. Barnum, part King Kong,
Part Chucky doll (the hair, the smile),
Part "buffoon," say Cheech and Chong.

Next up was Rome. Pope Francis sat
As in a deep hypnotic trance,
Smiling like the Cheshire Cat.
The Donald gave his watch a glance

And said, "It's late, I'm outta here,
I got a date in Brussels, France...
Or is it Germany? Their beer
Is great. I pledge to shift my stance

On climate change and global peace,
And even refugees. Our staffs
Can mention in our joint release
We had a great time, lots of laughs."

The NATO Summit was a matter
Of a different stripe and hue.
"This man's madder than a hatter!"
Sniped a minister or two.

Envoys had been told to plan
To keep their statements brief, to fit
The Donald's short attention span.
"Two minutes max. Get used to it."

Montenegro's P.M. felt
Trump's elbow as he bullied past.
The President of France was dealt
A handshake that was hard and fast.

When told his speech went over like
A lead balloon, he sneered and said,
"You guys are losers. Take a hike.
NATO, when I'm through, is dead."

The Donald's fabulous Grand Tour
Came off as scripted. Jeez Louise,
He even found a short-term cure
For chronic foot-in-mouth disease.

The Magic Orb

*At the palace of Crown Prince Mohammed
bin Salman Al Saud, ruler of Saudi Arabia*

He placed his tiny hands atop
The glowing orb and asked his host,
"After I do my belly flop,
How many virgins will I boast?"

"As many as you want," Al Saud
(No piker when it comes to lies)
Said, thinking, "How this whopping clod
Became the President defies

Imagination and belief!
But hey, for a hundred billion clams
I'll pick his pocket like a thief
And he can have his little lambs."

The Donald tried to calculate
How many virgins he could use
But after reaching twenty-eight
His frontal cortex blew a fuse.

Par for the Course

When not involved in campaign trips
Or formal duties of the POTUS,
Like watching CNN for slips
Or giving COVID experts notice,

He's found, most often, swinging clubs
On this golf course or that—enough
To make one wonder why, since flubs
Are known to land him in the rough.

In photos taken by the press,
He's either at the tee, or putting
Off the fairway through tall grass
Aboard his trusty cart, or strutting

Like a Leghorn cock across
The green to tip a "gimme" in—
The ball his caddy saw him toss
Up from a sand trap toward the pin.

He boasts a handicap that beats
The likes of Tiger Woods. His scores
Reflect deep-down beliefs: He cheats,
Tells lies about his lies, ignores

Two strokes or more on every hole.
There is no way to know the total,
But trust that winning is his goal.
[None of this is anecdotal.]

L'État, C'est Trump

As Alan Dershowitz now says,
There is no law above the Prez.
King Donald, as he'll soon be known,
Can flop upon his golden throne
And rule the universe by tweet
While toadies kneel and kiss his feet.
Once Moscow Mitch has scratched his itch,
He'll strategize, without a glitch,
On possibilities for graft
And giving Democrats the shaft.

Ways & Means

GoFundMe is the perfect way
To get Americans to pay
For walls or wars or golfing trips
Or lavish meals, including tips,
And while we're at it, money spent
On tax breaks for the One Percent.
We'll see how fast the platforms fill
When those in favor foot the bill.

IV

*"I went to an Ivy League school.
I'm highly educated. I know words,
I have the best words."*

O Commandant! My Commandant!

The poop deck on the Ship of State
Is knee deep with the sticky stuff
That pours forth from our Potentate
When he deigns to pontificate
On complex topics off the cuff.

His brain spins like a billiard ball
And ricochets between the beams.
His tweets hold followers in thrall,
His rants scorn law and protocol,
And not a thought means what it seems.

He's hanging by his fingernails.
The quartermaster rings eight bells!
He has an ill wind in his sails
And everything he touches fails,
But on he plunges, through the swells.

He sees his destiny fulfilled!
He'll kill Obamacare, and crown
His head with laurel leaves, and gild
His Oval Office throne, and build
His wall before the ship goes down.

The Tao of D'oh

Our clueless Commander-in-Chief
Wants intelligence briefings kept brief,
Using words short and sweet
That will fit in a tweet—
It boggles beyond disbelief!

Six Pack

The Don believes that he should win
A Nobel Prize, or five or six.
In Physics, he has shown that spin,
When issued from a loony bin,
Can pulverize our politics.

In Chemistry, he's proved that air
Can hold more carbon than we thought.
In Medicine, the wear-and-tear
He's heaped upon Obamacare
Gives private plans a booster shot.

In Economics, he has shone,
Imposing tariffs left and right
For reasons only he alone
Can fathom (if he has a bone
To pick, you're in his line of sight).

In Literature, no one alive
Or dead and in his grave competes
In volume or in hyperdrive
With Prexy Number Forty-five
When he taps out his twisted tweets.

The Peace Prize looms just out of reach.
He's asked dear Vladimir to dance,
And they've found novel ways to breach
Time-honored protocols; impeach
The Don, and peace will stand a chance.

On Giving the Wall the Gate

Trump wants to build The Wall. We know
This to be true, from all accounts.
The estimates are in. They show
The cost will vary, with amounts

From one-point-six on up to five
Bazillion dollars—all to please
The only humanoid alive
Who wants the thing. Analyses

All show there is no need to build
A wall along our southern border.
Trump wants his fantasy fulfilled.
His clear delusional disorder

Should make his Senate allies squirm.
They have to answer to the folks
Back home. The turning of the worm
Is nigh—his heavy-handed hoax

Will strip them to their undershorts
And shine a light on their neglect
Of issues of import. Their warts
Will multiply. Who'd re-elect

A profligate who spends our dough
Like water and ignores our needs?
Trump seeks to deal a lethal blow
To sanity—as if his deeds

To date show any common sense.
If Congress fails to scratch his back,
He'll hold all spending in suspense!
This latest ego-fed attack

On rationality should be
Enough to make Mitch reassess,
Though Mueller's probe should hold the key
To cleaning up the Trumpster's mess.

Yodeling All the Way

> "We got climbers. We had twenty mountain climbers. That's all they do—they love to climb mountains. They can have it. Me, I don't want to climb mountains. But they're very good, and some of them were champions. And we gave them different prototypes of walls, and this was the one that was hardest to climb."
> —Donald Trump, Leader of the Free World

When twenty climbers went to test
My wall, one section proved the best.
This was the prototype I chose,
The one that snookered alpine pros.

My message here is crystal clear:
Only the most skilled mountaineer
Can scale my wall's imposing face,
My tribute to the master race.

If you believe this latest tale
You'll love the bridge I have for sale.

Double Whammy

> "You look at other countries where they do it differently and it's a whole different story. I was with the President of Finland and he said we are a forest nation. He called it a forest nation. And they spend a lot of time on raking and cleaning and doing things, and they don't have any problem."
> —Donald Trump, on why Finland doesn't have wildfires

The Finns have given us a take
On how to keep our woods from burning.
All we have to do is rake
Dead leaves and twigs, and keep returning

So all our forest floors stay neat
And clean for our complete enjoyment.
The Donald's found, as he will tweet,
A cure for chronic unemployment.

Breaking Wind

The Donald never understood
That wind is clean, and pure, and good.
Although he's not a windmill fan,
He's studied them and therefore can
Declare with clear autonomy
How bad a wind economy
Would be. Windmills are known to spew
Tremendous fumes and residue,
A skill in which he's also versed.
He claims our tiny world is cursed—
A monster carbon footprint looms—
If we continue spewing fumes
And "everything" into the air
That Germany and China share.
In keeping with his climate goal,
He stuffs our stockings full of coal.

The Devil's in the Details

Donnie's plan to buy Greenland
Was destined to fail,
Most of all because Greenland
Was not up for sale.

You could hear Mitch McConnell
And Paul Ryan grouse:
He'd not bothered to brief
Either Senate or House.

And was Denmark consulted?
Did diplomats speak?
Did the White House Press Corps
Find itself up the creek?

Had the Treasury folks
Figured out an amount?
Was the funding to come
From his own bank account?

Had The Donald forgotten
To swallow his meds?
People everywhere laughed,
While the Danes scratched their heads.

Making Mockery Great Again

The metaphors that best suggest
The White House mousetrap set to snap
On Donald and his star-crossed nest—
The fast fuse in the blasting cap

Tucked tightly where the sun don't shine,
The corner where he paints the floor,
The limb he's out on, his "red line"—
Are nothing next to what's in store.

The lid is off Pandora's box,
And all the wags who pit their wits
Have kettled like a flock of hawks
To flaunt their tweets and YouTube skits.

Who says America's not great?
With howlers, bloopers, scoffs, and gaffes,
The man our nation loves to hate
Has dished us up a million laughs.

Vicente for Presidente

Vicente Fox is quite a card.
You might call him a Joker.
He caught The Donald off his guard
And scored a take-down, no-holds-barred,
Armed only with a poker.

He jabbed him once—he jabbed him twice—
His barbs were sharp as skewers.
La Broma En Naranja's price?
Vicente diced his every vice
And cracked up scads of viewers.

If Russia's Putin can conspire
To vilify poor Hillary,
Why can't a Mexican spitfire
Who calls the flake a flaming liar
Lock Donald in a pillory?

[*La Broma En Naranja:* The Orange Joke]

The Wily Gerrymander

The Gerrymander, like the Slithy Tove,
Is slightly slimy (think of Karl Rove)
And angular, an ersatz Etch A Sketch
Conception rendered by a scurvy wretch
Shape-shifting as he draws a line between
Hard-to-starboard types and those who lean
To port, thus making sure the hoi polloi
Stay in their place—an airtight, ironclad ploy
To maintain order in an otherwise
Untidy world, where Mome Raths jeopardize
The Borogoves, and one-percenters scratch
Their itch for riches with a Bandersnatch.

V

"I am a very stable genius."

"What I Love" by Donnie Trump

I love locking kids in cages,
Kissing up to right-wing thugs,
Laughing at starvation wages,
Pumping up the cost of drugs.

I love shutting down the poor,
Cutting taxes for the rich,
Acting like an utter boor,
Branding forceful women "Bitch."

I love boasting Russian friends,
Bedding bimbos by the score,
Reaping Mitch's dividends,
Drumming up a global war.

I love watching cable news,
Taking cues from Hannity,
Hurling racist slurs at Jews,
Wallowing in vanity.

I love ogling shapely buns,
Handing jobs to nincompoops,
Shielding creeps who covet guns,
Praising neo-fascist groups.

I love preaching to the flock,
Forcing farmers on the dole,
Spouting lies and doubletalk,
Deepening the fiscal hole.

I love stiffing diplomats,
Blocking scans of tax returns,
Bashing left-wing Democrats,
Golfing while the planet burns.

Shaking Hands

When Donald Trump first met Theresa May
He clasped her outstretched hand and pulled her tight
Mumbling the sorts of nothings he might lay
On bright-eyed bimbos in the dead of night.

He pulled the same faux pas with Shinzō Abe,
Though *faux pas's* absent from The Donald's lexis.
It's not like calling someone *kemosabe*
Or *pardner* or *compadre* in West Texas.

A body language expert boiled it down
To alpha male behavior. Power and sex.
The pull, the pat, the smirk, the circus clown
Burlesque, the slow withdrawal, meant to vex.

He added Netanyahu to the notches
Carved where he keeps track of crude behavior.
(He fills in scorecards when he's groping crotches.)
Republicans are calling him their Savior.

Little Donnie's Really Big Parade

If Macron and Putin can swagger their stuff
And even the Rocket Man gets his parade,
Why can't Little Donnie play Billy Goat Gruff?
In terms of pure bluster, he's equally tough
And wants the whole world to be freaking afraid.

He needs to pump up his deflated libido
To show humankind that his button is bigger.
He hopes he can rise above cries of *Stupido!*
By making debasement the crux of his credo
And gagging the people who giggle and snigger.

Bombs Away

Google "idiot" and guess whose face
Pops up, in Images, at Number One?
Little Donnie's! Same with Second Place
As well as Third and Fourth and Fifth. What fun!

Google's algorithm is to blame.
It does a lot of nifty little things
But can be twisted in a kind of game
Where rings of shifty people pull the strings.

Reddit's right-wing forum tags nonstop.
On Reddit, smears and lies "are fine to post."
Bill Clinton, tagged with "rapist," hit the top
Of Google's list. "Free speech," their people boast.

But Little Donnie couldn't wait to vent,
So even though it's Reddit's fault, for Pete's
Sake, he takes aim at Google with intent
To bomb them to oblivion with tweets.

A Quartet of Quatrains

They're Coming to Take Us Away

My older friends, I must confess,
Are scared down to their sneakers.
They've heard about, with great distress,
Trump's vow to smoke out leakers.

Trump Orders U.S. to Mine the Moon

The Donald wants to mine the moon
For all its worth. He fears Chinese
Cartels or some Blue State tycoon
Will seize his rightful prize—green cheese!

Run, Michael, Run

My best advice to Michael Cohen: Flee.
This latest tape has turned The Donald blue.
Eyeball to eyeball with reality,
He's bound to wonder, "What would Putin do?"

Hello? Anybody Home?

I think that I shall never see a Pence
Who comes across so absolutely dense
That he would choose to sit upon his hands
While everybody else applauds and stands.

The Donald Prepares Coast Guard Academy Cadets for the Post-Reality World by Making a Martyr of Himself for His Shabby Treatment at the Hands of Dishonest Mainstream Media

No politician in the world
Has suffered slings and arrows hurled
With such ferocity by foes
On mainstream network TV shows.

No pol in all the universe
Has suffered under such a curse,
From pre-reality Big Bang
To post-Obama *sturm und drang*.

No politician—no, not one—
Has been so thoroughly undone,
So flattened like a plate of peas,
And that's including Socrates.

A Trio of Limericks with Titles

Common Threads

The Red Queen cries, "Off with his head!"
Trump yells, "I will sue you!" instead.
Fabricating disputes,
He then fashions lawsuits
Designed to drape rivals in dread.

Crowd Control

Trump's Tulsa event was designed
As a poke in the nation's behind,
But his malice and spite
Weren't enough to excite
The cult of the deaf-dumb-and-blind.

"They Don't Like Me" (Hold the Tears)

The White House considers it strange
That the High Court is thinking long-range.
It isn't that SCOTUS
No longer likes POTUS,
They're doing their job for a change.

Top Priority

> "Trump campaign seeks new nickname for Biden."
> —*National Review*

I'm spending all my frickin' time
On campaign issue Number One—
Not COVID-19, tough on crime,
Or immigration, things I've done.

No way! I need a catchy name,
Since "Sleepy Joe" no longer rings
A bell with voters. It's too tame.
I want an epithet that stings!

I pound the Oval Office floor.
How do I stamp him? Loser? Sucker?
What's mean and nasty to the core?
I know who'll know—my buddy Tucker!

Little Donnie's Very Bad Dream

The Don denounces vote-by-mail,
Believing it's a vicious plot
To guarantee that Ds prevail.
The gerrymander won't mean squat.

And what about suppression laws
That Rs worked years to put in place?
Dear Leader fears he'll hear guffaws
If voters toss him on his face.

Hair Apparent

Trump's coif is a study in weird,
Like an upside-down cake or a beard,
Or a fur muff installed
To disguise where he's bald,
Or a gooseberry thicket unsheared.

VI

*"The worst thing a man can do
is go bald."*

Doctor No

> *Dr. Harold Bornstein served as Trump's personal physician from 1980 to 2018.*

Despite the size of Donnie's gut,
The Doc told us he's in good health.
The deal? He keeps his big mouth shut
And gets a cut of Donnie's wealth.

His first report used glowing terms
(*Extraordinary*, for example),
But didn't bog us down with germs
Or things like Donnie's urine sample.

His adjectives caused some to raise
Strong doubts about the authorship,
Since Little Donnie's known to praise
Himself—a lavish ego trip.

One day the Doc turned tattletale,
Said Donnie wrote what he had signed.
Did Donnie threaten to impale
The Doc, or paddle his behind?

No way. He sent his minions round
To gather up the doctor's files.
"A raid!" the doctor yelled. Don ground
His teeth, but told the Doc, all smiles,

That such a move was protocol.
The Doc had pitched two strikes; the third
Was launched, an inside knuckleball
That hurled toward Donnie like a turd.

The Doc leaked word that Donnie took
A drug that spurs the growth of hair
And treats enlarged prostates. Don shook
His fists, enraged, and filled the air

With epithets that laced Fox News
Reports with bleeps. (The Don recalled
The late-night TV talk show schmooze
Suggesting he was going bald.)

Doc either was a hippie dude
Bound by his Hippocratic Oath
Or didn't fancy getting screwed
By Don the Super Con, or both.

He said he didn't understand
The fuss. "A lot of guys, I think,
Have problems with their prostate gland."
Of course, he said it with a wink.

Doctor Maybe

Dr. Ronny Jackson served as Physician to the President and Deputy Assistant to the President until Trump nominated him as Secretary of Veterans Affairs in March 2018. A report by the Department of Defense Inspector General revealed that Jackson drank alcohol to excess and took sleeping pills while on duty, and complimented a female subordinate on her "tits" and "ass" in front of other subordinates, among a long list of charges. A year later, playing his Trump card in a red state, he was elected to the U.S. House of Representatives.

His nomination didn't cut
The mustard or the onions, but
Republicans in Texas saw
A candidate who mocks the law
And sandwiched him between the buns
Of troglodytes who worship guns
And those who think abortion sucks.
His lack of ethics drew big bucks
From billionaires who share his views
On sex and sleeping pills and booze.

Doctor Yes

Dr. Sean Conley served as Trump's White House physician from 2018 to 2021.

Not one to let a grim fact slip
Between his stiffened upper lip
And that which overlays his chin,
The Donald's latest doctor's in
The doghouse for his flip-flops on
A simple question: Was The Don
Hooked up to a machine? He lied
And then, to rub it in, supplied
An alibi the Liars Club
Would dub a monumental flub:
"We keep the public worry-free
By sparing them the truth. The key
To bliss is ignorance. What good
Is served if people understood
How close their president had come
To dying like some homeless bum,
Some migrant in a border camp...
But I digress. Our guy's a champ.
We can't let him be seen as weak,
And so we practice doublespeak."
[The Doc insinuated this,
Including ignorance is bliss.]

Is Donnie Really Bald on Top?

For someone who denies the science
Of everything from A to Z,
He puts a great deal of reliance
On hair-growth pharmacology.

On breezy days we see reflections
As sculpted hair lifts from his pate
And slowly settles back. Connections
Can be made here. Donnie's fate

Depends on one clear-cut equation
That pits his fear of growing bald
Against his love of tax evasion,
Lying, cheating…. Who's appalled

By anything he tweets on Twitter
When his so-called facts are faux?
So much for Don, the heavy hitter—
No show, but loads and loads of blow.

U.S. and Russia Revive Cold War Game of Provocative Street Names

—Headline, *The New York Times*

It's not enough that Donnie tweets
Faux news. Now he's renaming streets
To make his buddy Putin burn
And dish up insults in return.

America's new battle cry,
"I know you are, but what am I?"
Reminds us that the Cold War games
We played with Russia—all the names

We hurled while standing toe to toe
Like Larry, Moe, and Curly Joe—
Were products of pubescent boys
Out wagging their atomic toys.

CNN Poll

Did or didn't Donald lie?
Nine percent give him the nod,
While ninety-one percent applaud
Old Glory, Mom, and Apple Pie,
The NSA, the FBI,
The NBA, the NFL, and God.

The nine percent say he will drain
The swamp, employ his business sense,
Fulfill his promise to dispense
With rules. Those with half a brain
Admit they're rich and hope to gain
A bigger share at no expense.

The ninety-one percent are split
On what it is they least admire
About a chief who likes to fire
Subordinates for counterfeit
Misdeeds, a flaming hypocrite
Who wallows in the muck and mire.

Some score his monumental lack
Of empathy and self-control,
Some shame his emphasis on coal
With solar, wind, and wave on track
To blunt the CO^2 attack
As Earth grows warmer, pole to pole.

The vast majority would laugh
To see him lift aloft and float,
Bleating like a billy goat,
Bloated as a fatted calf,
Out to sea, his epitaph:
Putin had me by the throat.

Vlad the Impaler

If Vladimir has got the goods
On Donald, as we're hearing,
Those tête-à-têtes with Russian hoods,
That talk of racketeering,

Suspicious deals where real estate
Was used to launder money,
Entrapments dangling girls as bait—
Who wouldn't find it funny

That Donald sets his foes ablaze
With equal sound and fury,
While heaping Vladimir with praise?
Let's leave it to the jury.

Meanwhile, in a Galaxy Far, Far Away...

My dearest darling Best Friend Vlad,
I'm calling just to say I'm glad
For all the help you've given me—
And now our buddy Flynn is free!

> *Bugger!* as the British say.
> *Cock-up! Nutter!* Hip hooray,
> Your henchman let your hit man loose—
> Why all the fuss? What's your excuse?

Comrade Vlad, you're not alone.
I've hit some snags. My golden throne,
My Mar-a-Lago dock, delayed.
Like you, I cancelled my parade.

> Dumb shit, you think you've got it bad?
> My plot just tanked. I'm hopping mad.
> I had the whole thing nailed down—
> President for life, you clown!

Don't worry, once the losers die
We'll both be back and flying high.
In confidence, if I may brag,
My reelection's in the bag.

> How can you be so bloody dull?
> I've tried to pound this through your skull—
> I may not get a second chance!
> And you would have me sing and dance?

You are the greatest, Vlad. First-class.
Your oligarchs will save your ass.
Calm down. I'll phone you later on—
And by the way, please call me Don.

The Coronavirus Conspiracy

The Russians say that Trump's to blame.
Corona's, after all, a crown,
And Donnie's thinking he'll proclaim
His place atop the Hall of Fame,
Tweeting while the house burns down.

He wouldn't dare blame Putin's crew.
Their oligarchs would not be glad.
They think disloyalty's a cue
To pull the plug and turn the screw.
Besides, the crown belongs to Vlad.

For Your Eyes Only

Dear Don,
You've gone and done some crazy things,
You and your crew of ding-a-lings.
My oligarchs begin to squawk.
Let's sit down, face to face, and talk.

> Dear Vlad,
> I'm glad I'm going to get a chance
> To dine and dance, and sing and prance,
> With all those sweetie pies I knew
> The last time I sat down with you.

Dear Don,
Come on, I'm serious this time.
If Mueller pins you with a crime
And those who own you wind up squeezed,
They're apt to be a bit displeased.

> Dear Vlad,
> My Dad, when he was in a fix,
> Would hook up with a bunch of chicks,
> And everybody would undress.
> What better way to deal with stress?

Dear Don,
Your swan song, at the end, will be
An unrepentant guilty plea.
To be successful as a crook,
You can't go acting like a schnook.

> Dear Vlad,
> So sad. I thought that we were pals.
> But will you still provide the gals?
> My all-time favorite is the spanker.
> I never found the words to thank her.

Trumpster Diving

While Mueller digs and sifts the dirt
From Trump's prodigious midden,
Screening every jot, alert
To what Trump thought he'd hidden—

Clues to who did what, and when,
Where all the bones are scattered,
Why souls were sold, and then, again,
How only Donald mattered—

Trump's buddy Vlad is grasping now
The folly of his blunder,
That it's too late to disavow
His ties to Blood and Thunder.

The Ho-Humness of Donald's Misdeeds

When Bill and Monica were hot
The coverage was round the clock.
The Trump-and-Russia tryst is caught
Between a hard place and a rock.

The media have Donald's tweets
To analyze before they choose
Whatever else there is that meets
The current acid test for news.

Reporters work for billionaires,
Which puts a yoke around their necks.
There's little interest in affairs
That don't dish up some sizzling sex.

So what if Donald rigged the vote
And danced as Russia pulled his strings?
He's wearing Reagan's Teflon coat
And Putin's Kevlar underthings.

Presidential Kiss-off

Dear Vladimir, my bosom buddy Vlad,
The Faux News media have found me out.
I fear my situation's looking bad.
My reelection chances are in doubt.

I've danced when you have pulled my strings,
Turned allies into foes and foes to friends,
Stirred discontent at home, and other things.
Your rubles have paid handsome dividends.

I may request asylum—are you on?
Your faithful and devoted servant, Don

    Dear Donald, Comrade Don as you prefer,
    I take it you are seeking my support.
    Your media are right—I must concur.
    I'd like to help, but I'm a little short.

    The world is being primed for Russian rule.
    My oligarchs and I have work to do.
    We'll find another dupe who'll play the fool.
    Truth is, we have no further use for you.

    No hair spray, dressed in orange—be of good cheer
    In prison! *Dasvidaniya,* Vladimir

A Tale of Two Tyrants

When Netanyahu doffed his crown
Few people even knew it.
Said Don to Bibi, "Why the frown?"
Said Bibi, "I just blew it."

He spoke of skipping out of town
And wondered if he'd rue it.
But Don was upbeat. "Settle down.
We own the courts, so screw it."

Meathead

The president's son-in-law thinks
The loss of his privileges stinks—
The norms are to blame,
Not his confidence game
Or his foreign emolument links.

VII

"All the women on The Apprentice flirted with me, consciously or unconsciously. That's to be expected."

The Devil's Apprentice

Ms. Omarosa has The Donald reeling
On the ropes. She lands an uppercut,
A right cross, then a flurry to the gut.
His tweets about the matter are revealing.
She's outmaneuvered him to where he's dealing
With a deep fear of defeat. She's kicking butt,
While he can't figure out exactly what
To say or do except to hit the ceiling.

Some people go through life intimidating
Lesser souls until resistance crumbles.
The Donald finds this match excruciating,
Knowing it's all over if he stumbles.
This Apprentice learned her lessons well,
Toe-to-toe against the Boss from Hell.

The Dog Daze of August

Have you noticed how Donald's demeanor has changed
Ever since Omarosa punched holes in his vanity?
He's evolved from defiant to downright deranged,
With his tweets showing inklings of outright insanity.

First a book, then a tape, then a promise of more
Set him back on his heels. While his sycophants huddled,
Discussing how best they might settle the score,
The Donald just went about acting befuddled.

The United States Cheerleader Squad

The military's newest branch
Is seeking young female recruits.
Fox News predicts an avalanche
Of femmes with stunning attributes.

The President himself will choose
The candidates who score the best
In lengthy private interviews.
Then those who pass the swimsuit test

Will train at Mar-a-Lago's gym
To march in lockstep, two by two,
And sing the USCS Hymn:
"Red lips, white skin, and eyes of blue…"

Stormy Blows the Whistle

Trump paid his blonde porn star a tidy sum
For (as he puts it) "sitting on her bum"
While he watched CNN and *Fox & Friends*
And YouTube hotties doing deep knee bends.

He delved into her "knowledge of affairs,
Domestic or whatever, no one cares,"
To see if she agreed that Kim Jong-un
Was Number Two and he was Number One.

She volunteered to join his private staff,
But General Kelly cautioned, "Folks will laugh.
The evil media will turn the screws
On White House sources for their interviews."

"She'll blow my alibi! The working class
Will think my main concern's a piece of ass
When we all know it's their welfare," Trump said.
"But off the record, she was great in bed!"

Stormy Blather

The SLAPP suit just filed by Trump's lawyer,
In his latest attempt to destroy her,
Shows that Stormy's a pain
In the President's drain
And she's sticking it to his employer.

Ménage à Trois

The Don drops Wednesday's cable news,
Whose anchors show him no respect,
And watches Roseanne put the screws
To alt-left losers who refuse
To bend their knees and genuflect.

Her sister, Jackie, plays the fool,
The left-wing bird with half a brain
Who perches on her ducking stool
While making faces, dribbling drool,
And croaking like a whooping crane.

Poor Dan is caught between two rocks,
The Wealthy and the Working Class.
One fries his eggs and darns his socks,
The other flocks with chicken hawks
And doesn't know his ass from grass.

Dan gives the one he lives with breaks,
Tiptoeing down the center stripe,
Ignoring boring bellyaches.
Roseanne and Don? A pair of flakes
Who share their love affair with hype.

Polish Two-step

When Agata Kornhauser-Duda
Gave Donald a quickie saluda,
After greeting his wife
As the love of her life,
He scowled like a scorned barracuda.

Making America Itch Again

Paddy Power, the Irish betting house,
Is setting odds at ten-to-one that soon
Exterminators will remove the louse

Responsible for all the bodies strewn
About the Oval Office, down the stairs
And out across the lawn. The honeymoon

Was over when the flea-brained rake raised hairs
On everybody's arms and necks, from aides
And unpaid interns to the billionaires

Who pull the strings. But then when White House maids
Walked out en masse, the men in black swept in,
Replete with neat haircuts, designer shades

And shoulder-holstered gats. Even his kin,
The little nits who wallow in the dough
They need to show the losers how to win,

Are tempted by the odds—see how they grow!
No telling what will happen when his spouse
Is shown the Golden Piddle video.

VIII

"I love the poorly educated."

Whiteboards from Hell

Steve Bannon's nasty White House whiteboards boast
A panoply of panaceas, most
Of which are cures without diseases, such
As "Pull the plug on gray-haired grannies." Much

Of what he wants to do would break the law.
His fix? Rewrite the law to fit the flaw,
Assured that Congress will jump through his hoop
Because the foxes own the chicken coop.

He wants to build the border wall and then
Force Mexico to shriek, "Hell no!" again,
So he can shrug and say, "Oh well, we tried.
The media will whimper that we lied,

But people take that fact in stride. We've won
The propaganda battle, hit-and-run.
Like cattle in a feedlot, every sap
And sucker in the land's caught in our trap."

Manafort's Manifest Millions

> "Paul Manafort Is Living Proof
> That Money Can't Buy Style"
> —Headline in *Esquire*

Whatever prompted him to get
An ostrich leather jacket?
Was it to show he's out of debt
And in an upper bracket?

Or was it more to catch the eyes
Of kingpins in the racket,
To shout it out, I'm with you guys
An' got the dough to back it!

His loot poured in from overseas
As fast as he could stack it.
Then Mueller sparked an asset freeze.
Poor Manafort can't crack it.

A Trio of Bobbleheads

Loosey Goosey

The President, we've ascertained,
Speaks loosely and is unrestrained.
As Speaker Ryan has explained,
His nibs was never POTUS-trained.

The Last Days of Pompeo?

Pompeo claimed The Donald had apprised him
Before rezoning ground considered State's,
Though skeptics clucked and Democrats chastised him
For losing track of places, names, and dates.

To Donnie: On Your Bottom Dwellers

Expunge the humanoids, the droids,
The doofuses, the ding-a-lings,
The dingleberries running things
Before they morph to hemorrhoids!

The Great Prevaricator

It soon may be against the law to laugh
At circus clowns who make outrageous claims—
The President on down, his White House staff,
Congressional Republicans.... The Donald blames

The media for mimicking the art
He's mastered: telling whoppers out of hand.
His every breath—his sneeze, his belch, his fart—
Is disingenuous to beat the band.

His temperamental fits and starts suggest
The Queen of Hearts in Lewis Carroll's *Alice*.
"Off with his head!" (as Comey will attest)
Smacks of despotism, spite, and malice.

Attorney General Sessions caused the burst
Of mirth that led a congressman to file
The bill outlawing mockery. The First
Amendment (hold the laughter) faces trial.

With one hand on the Bible, Sessions swore
To tell the truth, the whole truth, nothing but—
But like an automatic matador,
He waved his cape in one direction, cut

The other way, and didn't miss a beat.
(What else should we expect from acolytes
Trained at the Great Prevaricator's feet?)
The question had to do with civil rights;

His Senate confirmation panel heard
Him try to weasel out from under proof
That what he said was utterly absurd.
A flabbergasted gadfly raised the roof.

Rudy Giuliani

Top analysts are working round the clock
To ascertain if Giuliani's brain
Has turned to mushroom soup. To hear him talk,
You'd think he'd skipped off past the astral plane
And, crashing down, had landed on a rock.

Bad Penny

When Rudy Giuliani served
As mayor of New York,
His high esteem was undeserved.
In sum, he was a dork.

He brought his mistress home one day
To live at Gracie Mansion,
Much to his second wife's dismay.
He oversaw expansion

Of a half-baked war on crime.
You didn't spit for fear
You'd wind up fined and doing time,
Or sneeze if you were queer.

When 9/11 hit, he seized
The podium and basked
In lavish praise. He acted pleased
No matter what was asked

Because it meant another chance
To hog the microphone,
And do his little song and dance
Before the facts were known.

This latter trick he's maximized
As mouthpiece for The Don.
His viewers sit there mesmerized
By how he chatters on.

Integrity's put through the mill
Or blasted into space,
But yet again we get our fill
Of Giuliani's face.

Three-fingered Giuliani

Some twenty thousand daily
Keeps Rudy quibbling gayly,
Exceeding even Kayleigh.

He loves *My Cousin Vinny*,
The courtroom scene wherein he
Sinks to ignominy.

He's better cast as Bonnie,
With Clyde portrayed by Donnie—
Two pawns of QAnony.

Inartful Dodger

Did Donald Junior break the law
Or is this just another crock
Of hooey, caustic blah-blah-blah
From same-old same-old left-wing talk

Show hosts? As Utah's Orrin Hatch
Proclaimed with specificity,
"This Russia thing is just a batch
Of bunkum, no complicity

That I can see. Emails aside,
Forgetting Junior's own remarks
Admitting guilt, it's cut-and-dried
Codswallop from the faux news sharks."

Cervantes said the pudding's proof
Is in the eating. Hatch is right
(No pun intended): Stay aloof,
Pretend your case is watertight,

Let false facts fall like dominoes,
Too quick for checkers from the press
To stay abreast. Enlist the pros
To troll your innocence. Digress.

Conspiracy Theories

Sean Spicer was again all feet
As *Dancing with the Stars* wore on.
Not unexpectedly, a tweet
Was issued midway by The Don

To boost Sean's chances in the game.
Apparently the faithful yawned
And Sean was booted off in shame.
Poor Donnie shook his magic wand,

His phone, and wondered how the spell
Was broken. Was the show a sham?
Did Democrats raise holy hell?
Was he betrayed by Lindsey Graham?

Nightmare on Downing Street

Boris Johnson has a dream,
A take on Jean-Paul Sartre's *No Exit*—
Britain wakes up with a scream
To find there's no way out of Brexit.

Boris loves a right-wing flap
And deems himself iconoclastic—
Lunging toward a booby trap,
His ways and means supremely drastic.

Boris acts a lot like Trump:
Divide and conquer, sow confusion—
Bluff and bluster on the stump
With ample portions of delusion.

Boris speaks like Mr. Bean,
Pronouncements that bemuse, befuddle—
Genuflecting for the Queen,
Convincing her to cause a muddle.

Boris talks of making Trump
His trading partner after ditching
European countries—*thump!*—
Though Britain stands to lose by switching.

Boris learns guerilla tricks
From Breitbart's answer to Atilla—
Bannon, master of the fix,
Whose only flavor is vanilla.

Boris? That's a Russian name.
With Trump's Rasputin as his tutor—
An all-star in the Hall of Shame—
He's bound to be a persecutor.

The Dumb and the Dumber

Says billionaire Wilbur Ross,
Who seems to know less than his boss
About what it means
To scrape by on beans:
"Let them eat applesauce!"

Author's Notes

Politics is in my blood. In fact, my family tree boasts a number of public officeholders. Oregon Territorial Legislature. Oregon House and Senate. Clackamas County Board of Commissioners.

I got off to a slow start. In 1948, when I was 11, I wanted Truman to beat Dewey simply because my parents did. Classmates with Republican parents taunted me. I resisted the urge to return their taunts after Truman won. They wouldn't look me in the eyes, which was payback enough.

In 1956, as a sophomore at Oregon State University, I served as campus coordinator for the Pogo for President campaign, my first step up the political ladder. Three years later, as a senior at Portland State University, I joined the Young People's Socialist League.

Most of the guys were in it for the weed, the wine, and the women. All talk and no action, reminiscent of the People's Front of Judea in Monty Python's *Life of Brian*. Or was that the Judean People's Front?

In 1961, when I was assistant director of Oregon's tourism bureau, the publishers of *Sunset Magazine*, husband and wife, flew to Portland to interview me for a job as staff writer, on the recommendation of an editor I had assisted with a cover story on the Willamette Valley.

Things went well until, as we were parting, I was asked whether I had supported Eisenhower or Stevenson in the 1956 election. I said Eisenhower (I was two years shy of voting age in 1956, but my parents had voted for him). They asked me why, and, not knowing why, I said, meekly, "I like Ike?" A chill descended. The couple, I found out later, had co-chaired the national Stevenson campaign.

In 1968 I served as Oregon coordinator for the Chief Burning Wood for President campaign, but I had to resign after I went to work for an advertising and public relations agency and was promptly made Oregon coordinator for the Nelson Rockefeller for President campaign. It was time to get serious.

When New York City Mayor John Lindsay came to Portland, I whisked him here and there for appearances. He gave me an "official" necktie sprinkled with imperial seals and a lifetime pass to New York City subways. I felt I had arrived.

In 1970 I became assistant to Multnomah County Commissioner Mel Gordon. Eighteen months later I jumped to the Oregon House of Representatives as assistant to Majority Leader Les AuCoin. After the incredible 1973 session (Ds and Rs pulled together for the betterment of the state!), I freelanced on political campaigns, returning to the House in 1975 as assistant to Majority Leader Ed Lindquist.

Eighteen months after that, I went back to freelancing, juggling as many as nine political campaigns at a time, and writing all sorts of other stuff. (I had a habit of dropping in and out of full-time employment. At my 30th Oregon State reunion, I was awarded a cup for having changed jobs the most times: 16.)

In 1986 I joined the staff of Portland City Commissioner Dick Bogle for a spin as his speechwriter and media aide. I could (and might) fill a book with my experiences over the six years I spent at City Hall. I retired on January 1, 1993, returning to politics frequently, but in a new role: gadfly.

In the 1990s I joined with like-minded souls and fought tooth and nail to stop the encroachment of West Linn, Lake Oswego, and Tualatin, not to mention Clackamas County, into the bucolic Stafford Basin. I waged fierce op-ed battles in the *West Linn Tidings* and other papers. The basin remains undeveloped. One lesson I took away: Developers never sleep.

In 1997 I used every bit of knowledge and skill I'd acquired to stop a housing development on Canemah Bluff, just above the Falls of the Willamette, where my ancestors settled, and where many of them are buried. I won that battle. It's now Metro greenspace.

In 2000 I ran for state representative, not to win but to stop a pawn of the growth industry, a career politician with wide name familiarity, from waltzing in. I raised and spent less than $2,000. Relying on my Voters Pamphlet statement, I took 40 percent of the vote in the primary. My opponent lost in the general election.

A footnote: The local chapter of the League of Conservation Voters dubbed me an "environmental warrior" for saving Canemah!

In the years that followed, I worked as a volunteer on local campaigns, an enjoyable pastime, though things turned serious in 2015 when the candidate I favored for West Linn mayor decided not to approve a print ad I cooked up because he didn't wish to "go negative."

His opponent, a member of the city council, had convinced the public he was an educator (he taught night courses at a local university) when in fact he was chief financial officer for several development companies. I registered a political action committee with the secretary of state, raised just enough money to pay for several ads in the *Tidings,* and went to work. My candidate won.

I've won more contests than I've lost. One highlight: Bob Straub's win over two veteran campaigners, Attorney General Jim Redden and Senate President Betty Roberts, in the 1974 primary race for Oregon governor.

The take-away: My political involvement through the years has served basic principles of democracy. Win or lose, I accepted the will of the people, and never lied or tried to pull the wool over voters' eyes.

I'm pleased as punch with this book. It gives me a sense of being in the fight to protect and preserve America's great experiment in representative democracy from Trump-addled Republicans bent on installing the pompous bloviator as president for life, with his feckless offspring waiting in the wings to take over when he pops.

Join me in laughing at the clowns. It'll do you good.

About the Author

When not tilting at environmental, social, and political windmills, David Hedges has spent the past 63 years writing, first as a journalist, then as a public relations practitioner and editor, then as an advertising copywriter and producer, and then as a political writer and aide, all the while churning out poems, essays, and works of fiction. He has published eight books, including *Petty*  *Frogs on the Potomac* (1997), a poke at America's power base in rhymed verse; *A Funny Thing Happened on My Way to a Geology Degree* (2011), detailing, in verse, his escape to Greenwich Village six months shy of a degree and a commission in the Navy; *Prospects of Life After Birth: Memoir in Poetry and Prose* (2019), a chronicle of his early adventures; and finally, in 2021, *The Changer,* a novel based on the Interior Salish myth of the Change, marking the end of this world and the beginning of the next. He has served on the Oregon Cultural Heritage Commission board since 1988, and co-founded, with State Librarian Jim Scheppke and Poet Laureate Lawson Inada, the Oregon Poetry Collection at the University of Oregon's Knight Library. He served for 24 years on the Oregon Poetry Association board, six as president, founding and editing *Verseweavers,* OPA's annual anthology of prize poems, and creating the Oregon Student Poetry Contest, now in its 23rd year. At the 2003 Oregon Book Awards, he received the Stewart H. Holbrook Literary Legacy Award for his contributions to the state's literary life. He lives in Oregon City, Oregon, where his pioneer ancestors settled in the mid-1800s. View samples of his work at david.hedges.name.

About the Artist

Raised on an island in the Pacific Ocean, Jim Agpalza now lives outside Portland, Oregon, where he works as a freelance illustrator, cover artist, character designer, and storyboard artist. His work has appeared in a multitude of formats, including cartoons, books, slot machines, comics, and T-shirts. He is the co-creator and character designer of the animated show *Spacefish,* the novel *Fantastic Earth Destroyer Ultra Plus,* and the comic book *Crusader of Sin.* He has illustrated works by many authors, including Theodore Sturgeon and Isaac Asimov, and book covers for such acclaimed authors as Shane McKenzie and Edward Lee, and for Eraserhead Press, Deadite Press, and Lazy Fascist. View his artwork at jimagpalza.com.

Midnight in Moscow (3/2022)

Dear Comrade Don, feel free to blame
The war on Biden. Say it's bad.
But if you're smart you'll keep my name
Out of it. Your buddy, Vlad

www.ingramcontent.com/pod-product-compliance
Lightning Source LLC
Chambersburg PA
CBHW070918080526
44589CB00013B/1356